Dorothy Van Woerkom, the series editor for I CAN READ A BIBLE STORY, is no stranger to children's books.

Her first, *Stepka and the Magic Fire*, received the Catholic Press Association award for best religious children's book of 1974. *Becky and the Bear*, a book for beginning readers, and *The Queen Who Couldn't Bake Gingerbread* were both Junior Literary Guild selections. Ms. Van Woerkom has written several other books for Concordia, including *Wake Up and Listen*, an inspirational retelling of the passion story.

Aline Cunningham is the series illustrator for I CAN READ A BIBLE STORY. She is the author

and illustrator of the successful CATERPILLAR book series, published by Concordia. Her artwork has appeared in numerous publications including *Woman's Day, Better Homes and Gardens,* and *McCall's* magazines. A native of St. Louis, Ms. Cunningham has received 5 gold medals from the St. Louis Art Directors Club.

DANIEL,
WHO DARED

DANIEL, WHO DARED

Daniel in the Lions' Den for Beginning Readers

Daniel 1:1-8; 6 FOR CHILDREN

by Mary Blount Christian
illustrated by Aline Cunningham

I CAN READ A BIBLE STORY
Series Editor: Dorothy Van Woerkom

Publishing House
St. Louis

FOR·RAY BROEKEL WITH GRATITUDE

Concordia Publishing House, St. Louis, Missouri
Copyright © 1977 Concordia Publishing House
MANUFACTURED IN THE UNITED STATES OF AMERICA

Library of Congress Cataloging in Publication Data

Christian, Mary Blount.
    Daniel, who dared.

    (I can read a Bible story)
    SUMMARY: Tells the story of Daniel in the lions' den.
    1. Daniel, the prophet—Juvenile literature.
2. Bible. O.T.—Biography—Juvenile literature.
[1. Daniel, the prophet. 2. Bible stories—O.T.]
I. Cunningham, Aline. II. Title.
BS580.D2C47   224'.5'09505   77-6412
ISBN 0-570-07325-1
ISBN 0-570-07319-7 pbk.

Daniel was a Jew.

When he was a boy in Judea,

his country went to war

with the country of Babylon.

Judea lost the war.

Daniel was taken from his family
and brought to Babylon.
He learned to read and to write
the words of these people.
He learned their customs.

When Daniel became a man,
he worked for the king
of Babylon.
But he never forgot
the laws of God.

He would not eat food
from the king's table.
He would not drink the king's wine,
because the king prayed
to stone gods.

And three times each day
Daniel went to his room to pray.
He would not pray to the gods
of Babylon.

King Darius had many leaders
to help him rule the country.
The most important leaders
were three chief governors.
Daniel was one of the chief governors.
He was the best of the three.

King Darius was pleased
with Daniel's work.
He wanted to put him in charge
of all his business.
The other two governors
were very jealous.

One day these two governors were
walking together in the palace.
Their footsteps rang
against the tile floors.
"I have heard that Daniel
will be placed over us,"
said the older governor.
"The king thinks Daniel is
better than we are."

"Why does the king want HIM
to have all the power?"
shouted the younger governor.
"We must get rid of him,"
they decided. "Daniel must die!"

They thought for a moment.

Then one said to the other,

"The king likes Daniel.

Daniel never does anything wrong.

He obeys all the laws.

We need a new law.

We need a law

that Daniel will NOT obey!"

The younger man nodded his head.

"Let us call the leaders together

before the king," he said.

When the leaders came,

the young governor told them secretly,

"Daniel is too powerful.

He must be stopped.

"Daniel will not obey
a law against his God," he said.
"We have a plan that will
turn the king against Daniel."
Everyone agreed.

They all went to see the king.

"Long live King Darius!" they cheered.

"Oh, great King,"

began the older governor,

"We all want a new law

that will prove who loves you."

The king smiled.

The two governors moved closer
to the king.
One said boldly,
"Tell the people that for 30 days
they must not pray to any god.
They must pray only to you.
Anyone who breaks this law
will be put in the den
with the lions."

King Darius did not know
that this was a trick.
He said, "If you think this law
is a good law,
then I will make it."
And King Darius made the law.

"Can this law be changed?"

asked one of the leaders.

"No," said the king.

"Once this law is made,

not even I, the king,

can change it."

The two governors smiled at each other.

They went away

to spy on Daniel.

They found him in his room,

praying to God.

The wicked governors hurried back

to tell the king.

King Darius looked frightened.

"When I made this law, I did not know

that it would hurt Daniel!"

"But Daniel disobeys you," they said.

"You must throw him to the lions!"

"You made this law, oh, King,"
the young governor said.
"You cannot change it now.
Daniel must die."

King Darius was very angry.

He sent everyone away.

He walked up and down the room.

He worried all day.

"What can I do?" he cried.

"My governors have tricked me.

What a fool I have been!

I don't want Daniel to die!

But I cannot change the law."

His governors wanted an answer.

Finally, the king sent for Daniel.

"It is true," Daniel told the king.

"I pray to God

three times each day."

"Then ask your God to save you,"

King Darius said sadly.

The guards led Daniel

to the courtyard

where the lions were kept.

They rolled the great stone away

from the door of the den.

King Darius put his hand

on Daniel's shoulder.

"May your God

save you," he said.

Daniel shook his head.

"I am not afraid," he said.

"God is on my side."

Daniel walked into the den.

He saw red eyes in the darkness.

The guards rolled the stone

up to the door.

When Daniel looked back,

the sunlight was gone.

King Darius called to Daniel,

"We have put wax around the stone

to seal it tightly.

We have marked the wax

with the rings we wear.

No one can help you now

unless they break this seal."

"God does not need to break the seal
to help me," Daniel said.
But he could hear the lions
coming nearer.

King Darius walked slowly
back to his room.
He could still hear the lions
roaring and snarling.

The king could not eat or sleep.

He walked around the room,

listening to the lions.

Suddenly the roaring stopped.

"It is done!" King Darius moaned.

"The lions are quiet.

Daniel must be dead!"

He spent a sleepless night.

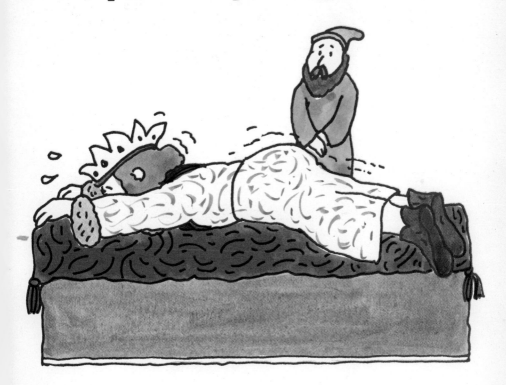

But it was not done!

God sent help to Daniel

Daniel felt stiff fur

as a lion brushed against him.

He felt its hot breath

as it snapped and snarled.

Daniel dropped to his knees.

"Oh, mighty God!" he prayed.

"Save me from these hungry lions.

Show the king and his people

that you are the living God!"

Suddenly, the roaring stopped.

Daniel stared at the lions.

They could not open their jaws!

They could not bite at him!

All night Daniel prayed.

Morning came.

King Darius called his guards

and hurried to the den.

"Daniel!" the king called.

"Are you safe?

Did your God save you?"

"I am safe," Daniel called out.

"God sent angels down

to shut the jaws of the lions!

They could not harm me."

The king's soldiers rolled away the stone.

Daniel came out into the sunlight.

King Darius threw his arms
around Daniel.
Now his tears were tears of joy.

King Darius pointed
at the wicked governors
and the other leaders.
"Now YOU must face the lions!"
he shouted. "And your false gods
will not save you."

The king smiled at Daniel.

"Oh, Daniel," he said.

"Your God is the true God."

"From now on,"
King Darius wrote to his people,
"you will pray
to the God of Daniel.
Only a true and living God
could have saved him
from the lions!"

ABOUT THE AUTHOR

Mary Blount Christian is the author of Concordia's new *Goosehill Gang* series. She has written more than a dozen other books, two of which have been on the Child Study Association's "Best Books of the Year" lists: *Devin and Goliath* and *No Dogs Allowed, Jonathan. Devin and Goliath* was Ms. Christian's first book for beginning readers, and it is now available to children who read in Braille. Ms. Christian is the creator of Public Television CHILDREN'S BOOKSHELF, a series of programs about children's books, their authors, and their illustrators. She lectures at colleges and universities, teaches creative writing in the Houston Community College, and is children's book critic for the Houston CHRONICLE. This is her third book in Concordia's I CAN READ A BIBLE STORY series.